LEVITICUS
A SELF-STUDY GUIDE

Irving L. Jensen

MOODY PRESS
CHICAGO

© 1967 by
THE MOODY BIBLE INSTITUTE
OF CHICAGO

Cover photo: St. Catherine's Garden near the Sinai mountains

ISBN: 0-8024-4482-2

1 2 3 4 5 6 Printing/EP/Year 95 94 93 92 91

Printed in the United States of America

Contents

Introduction

Leviticus is the third in a series of study manuals on the Pentateuch. The general procedures and methods of study suggested in the two previous books on Genesis and Exodus are followed here. The study of Leviticus will be most fruitful if these two earlier books have been studied first.

These lessons may be used either for individual or group Bible study. Incorporated in this self-study guide are various helps on analyzing the Bible chapter by chapter and paragraph by paragraph. Convinced that "the pencil is one of the best eyes," I have also given suggestions along the way as to how the student may record his analyses on paper.

Here are some suggestions that would apply in either case:
1. If any lesson seems too long for one unit of study, divide the lesson into two parts. Take on no more than you can study thoroughly.

2. It is important to read the Bible passage before beginning to study the lesson itself.

3. Always study with pencil and paper handy, jotting down important points as you study.

4. Look up and carefully study all Scripture references cited. The Bible is its own best commentary.

5. Keep in mind that effective Bible study involves:
OBSERVATION: What does the text say?
INTERPRETATION: What does the text mean?
APPLICATION: How does this apply to me today?
Notice that the key to correct interpretation is correct observation. This is why it is important to train the eyes to see what the Bible *actually says* and let the Bible *speak for itself.*

6. Depend on the Holy Spirit of God to guide and enlighten you in your study of the Scriptures.

Here are some suggestions to group leaders:

1. Urge the members of your class to diligently study the lesson at home before the meeting and to bring to class any written work called for by the lesson.

2. If possible, when teaching use enlarged copies (on cloth or paper) of the major charts and diagrams in this manual. The use of a chalkboard in class meetings is also highly recommended. When an overhead or opaque projector is available, the teacher can use this aid to great advantage.

3. At the beginning of each meeting, review the previous lesson, allowing the members of your group to participate.

4. Insist that the members think and study for themselves. Give each person ample opportunity to express ideas and ask questions. Do not lecture to the class.

5. Allow time for a summary at the end of the class period. Applications should be stressed at this time.

Lesson 1
Survey of Leviticus

Many of God's people avoid studying certain books of the Bible just as children turn down certain foods (e.g., the proverbial spinach) because they have not developed their tastes or appreciated the nourishing values of the victuals. Leviticus is one of the neglected books of the Bible for several reasons: (1) it appears dull because of its lack of action and plot (chap. 10 is a notable exception); (2) it appears heavy with hundreds of rules, regulations, and much repetition; and (3) many of its symbols appear difficult to interpret and apply.

But Leviticus is a most important book and should be studied. As a part of God's inspired Scriptures, it is "profitable for teaching, for reproof, for correction, for training in righteousness; that the man of God may be adequate, equipped for every good work" (2 Tim. 3:16-17, *New American Standard Bible*). What does Leviticus say that makes it profitable to man today?

1. It teaches basic truths about God and man.

2. It emphasizes the exceeding sinfulness of man and his estrangement from God.

3. By prefiguring the redemptive ministry of Christ it shows how man may be restored to God's fellowship.

4. Through the universal, timeless principles derived from its laws, the Christian may learn how to please God in his daily living.

For many reasons Leviticus is often considered the "gospel" of the Old Testament; it can be profitably studied in that light. After you have completed your study of this third book of the Scriptures you will agree that it holds a unique and important position in God's Word.

Our procedure of study in this lesson is first to acquaint ourselves with the background of the writing of Leviticus and then to get a view of the book as a whole.

I. THE BACKGROUND OF LEVITICUS

A. Name

It was the custom of the Jews to call each book of the Pentateuch by the first word of the Hebrew text. For Leviticus this was *wayyiqra*, meaning "and he called." The Greek Septuagint version, which was the first translation of the Old Testament, assigned the title *Leuitikon*, meaning "that which pertains to the Levites." The reason for such a title is obvious: much of the book concerns the ministry of the Levites or the priests, an important segment of the tribe of Levi (cf. Heb. 7:11). The Greek title was carried over into the Latin Vulgate as *Leviticus* and then adopted by the English Bible.

B. Author

The traditional view is that Moses was the author of this third part of the Pentateuch as well as the remainder of the Pentateuch. The internal and external evidence supporting this argument is overwhelmingly conclusive.

Christ explicitly ascribes the Pentateuch to Moses in Luke 24:44. In this passage Christ speaks of the three parts into which the Jews divided the Old Testament: "the law," "the prophets," and "the psalms," and clearly states that the law was of *Moses*. See also how Christ referred to Moses as the writer of Leviticus by comparing Matthew 8:2-4 with Leviticus 14:1-4. Fifty-six times in Leviticus it is explicitly stated that the Lord gave the laws to His people through Moses. That Moses wrote the instructions in a book is stated in Ezra 6:18.

C. Date

The passages in Exodus 40:17; Leviticus 1:1 and Numbers 1:1 are the basis for the following time setting of Leviticus.

God spoke the words of Leviticus during the first month of the second year after the Exodus. Just when Moses wrote down the words we cannot be sure, but he may have done so before the wilderness journey of Numbers began, around the middle of the fifteenth century B.C. (based on the 1445 B.C. date for the exodus from Egypt).

EXODUS FROM EGYPT	COMMANDMENTS GIVEN at SINAI	TABERNACLE (portable) CONSTRUCTED	LEVITICAL LAWS GIVEN	PREPARATION for WILDERNESS JOURNEY
Exodus 12:41	Exodus 19:1	Exodus 40:17	———	Numbers 1:1
Beginning of the new calendar	First year; Third month	Second year; First month; First day	Second year; First month	Second year; Second month; First day

D. Theme

The theme of Leviticus becomes clearer on comparing its contribution to the Pentateuch with that of the other four books. Notice the following comparisons:

GENESIS	EXODUS	LEVITICUS	NUMBERS	DEUTERONOMY
ORIGINS of the nation	DELIVERANCE of the nation	LIFE of the nation	TEST of the nation	REMINDERS to the nation
THEOCRACY BORN	THEOCRACY ESTABLISHED		THEOCRACY TESTED AND PREPARED FOR THE NEW HOME	
	COVENANT IS AMPLIFIED "Keep my covenant" to be a "peculiar treasure" "kingdom of priests" "holy nation" (Ex. 19:5-6)	LAWS ARE PRESCRIBED "which if a man do, he shall live in them: I am the Lord" (Lev. 18:5)		

Leviticus has a twofold theme, the way of God and the walk He demands. In the sense in which worship is both communion and dynamic living, Leviticus may thus be called the "Book of Worship."

II. A SURVEY OF LEVITICUS

A. The Structure of Leviticus

Before we look at the smaller sections of Leviticus, it is desirable to get a "skyscraper view" of the book. The following suggestions will guide you in such a study.

1. First scan the entire book, not lingering on details. As you read, jot down on a piece of paper a word or phrase that suggests the main contents of each chapter. Treat each chapter as a unit with these exceptions: let a new segment begin at 5:14 instead of at 5:1, and at 6:8 instead of at 6:1, and overlook the division at 7:1. Record these chapter titles on a horizontal chart like this:

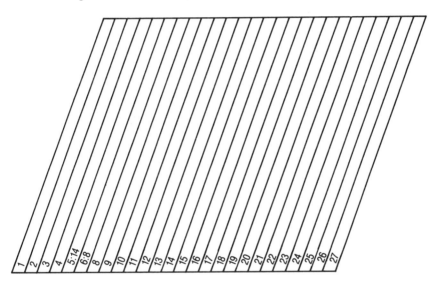

2. What were some of your impressions from this reading?

_____

_____

3. List key words and phrases and truths emphasized.

_____

_____

4. Did you observe any groupings of chapters with similar subject matter? For example, you probably noticed that the first seven chapters contain laws of the five offerings, set off from the next

section by 7:37-38. Indicate your own groupings on the chart you have already begun (above).

5. If Leviticus were divided into two main sections, where would the division be made? Indicate this on your chart.

6. Observe how many chapters begin with "And the Lord spake unto Moses, saying":

_____

_____

What do you learn from this?

_____

_____

7. Do any chapters in Leviticus seem to stand by themselves?

_____

Which chapter would you choose as a key chapter?

_____

Why does the subject matter of chapters 26 and 27 cause this portion to be placed at the end of Leviticus?

_____

_____

8. What is the prominent phrase of chapter 19?

_____

_____

9. From your general study of Leviticus, what items do you recall that are meant to be holy, or "clean"?

_____

_____

_____

10. What do you think were some major lessons that God was teaching the Israelites through the laws and regulations of Leviticus?

_____

_____

_____

_____

_____

LEVITICUS "YE SHALL BE HOLY"

CONSECRATION

CONSECRATION

Chapter		
1	BURNT	
2	MEAL	LAWS OF OFFERINGS
3	PEACE	
4	SIN	
5:14	TRESPASS	
6:8	LAWS of OFFERINGS	
8	AARON AND SONS ANOINTED	LAWS OF CONSECRATION OF PRIESTS
9	AARON'S OFFERINGS	
10	STRANGE FIRE	
11	EAT... TOUCH	
12	WOMAN CONCEIVE	LAWS OF PURITY
13	TEST of LEPROSY	
14	CLEANSING of LEPROSY	
15	UNCLEAN ISSUES	
16	ATONEMENT DAY	ATONEMENT
17	BLOOD SLAUGHTER	
18	UNCOVERING NAKEDNESS	HOLY PEOPLE
19	"I AM THE LORD"	
20	MOLECH	
21	PRIEST RULES	HOLY PRIESTS
22	PROFANE NOT	
23	HOLY CONVOCATIONS	HOLY TIMES
24	CONTINUALLY	
25	SABBATICAL YEAR AND JUBILEE	JUST RECOMPENSE
26	CONSEQUENCES	
27	VOWS	HOLY VOWS

THE WAY TO GOD

THE WALK WITH GOD

REDEMPTION

DAY OF ATONEMENT

RESTORATION

YEAR OF JUBILEE

HOLINESS

11

11. After you have answered the above questions on your own, study the accompanying outline chart of Leviticus.

Note the following:

(a) Leviticus may be divided into two main sections, the division being made at 18:1. Chapters 16 (day of atonement) and 17 (blood of sacrifice) serve as a climax to the first half of the book, showing *the way to God*. Read 18:1-5 and notice how these words introduce a new theme, that of doing and living, or *the walk with God*.
(b) The word "holy" is the key word of Leviticus (Strong's concordance shows its appearance in 90 places), and this truth is emphasized especially in the last half of the book. Note the outline: holy people, holy priests, holy times, just recompense, holy vows. Study these key verses on holiness: 11:44-45; 19:2 (we may consider this to be a key verse for Leviticus); and 20:7, 26. Compare the truths about holiness taught in Psalms 15:1-2; 24:3-4; Matthew 5:8; 1 John 1:6-7.

_____

_____

_____

_____

c. Observe that Leviticus opens with the exhortation to consecration (freewill offering) and closes on that same note (freewill vows).

B. Underlying Principles and Truths of Leviticus

Throughout your study of the hosts of *details* in Leviticus you will want to identify the underlying root truths in order to make present-day applications. The following list suggest some of the more important principles and root truths:
  1. The laws of Leviticus were given because of the immediate need of Israel to know how to worship God and how to live lives acceptable to Him from day to day. The symbols were picture lessons of spiritual truths.
  2. Leviticus also had a prophetic purpose, by way of types, speaking of the Person and ministry of Christ. This is the major Christian aspect of the book. When Leviticus was written, what was *type* for future generations was *symbol* for its contemporaries.
  3. All the laws and regulations designed by God and delivered from the Tabernacle (1:1) are purposeful.

12

4. Sinful man is estranged from the holy God.

5. The just penalty for sin is death through the shedding of blood, in which resides the life of the flesh.

6. God in His grace allows death of an *acceptable substitute* as payment for sin's penalty.

7. When man comes into fellowship with the holy God, he must live in the light of this new experience.

8. Offerings to God must be made willingly, in the spirit of obedience to His instructions.

9. God uses His ministers (in Leviticus, the priests) to bring men to Himself.

10. God is interested in the perennial cycle of man's living, illustrated by the divine calendar designed for Israel.

C. Relation of Leviticus to the New Testament

The sacrifices of Leviticus point to the supreme sacrifice of all history, Christ, the Lamb of God. The priests of Leviticus point to the Great High Priest, Jesus. The worshipers in Leviticus foreshadow the Christians of the New Testament. The symbols, types, and shadows found throughout this third book of the Bible find their objects in the New Testament. And of all the New Testament books, the epistle to the Hebrews is the most explanatory. (It would be well to read Hebrews before proceeding any further in the study of Leviticus.)

D. The Tabernacle: Scene of the Offerings

Study the layout of the Tabernacle areas shown on pages 11 and 12. It will be a great help if you can visualize the movements of the priests in the Tabernacle area as they performed their functions during the Levitical sacrifices. (For further light on this subject, consult a book on the Tabernacle.)

III. SUMMARY

Leviticus is the record of God's instructions to Israel as to how His people might have access to Him in worship and walk with Him in fellowship. The book has a vital message for today because the *blood*, the prominent truth of chapters 1-17, explains *why Christ was crucified*; and *holiness*, the prominent truth of chapters 18-27, tells us *why we are crucified with Christ*.

PLAN OF THE JEWISH TABERNACLE

DIMENSIONS (one cubit equals approximately 1½ feet)
- COURT—100 BY 50 CUBITS
- GATE—20 CUBITS
- TABERNACLE—30 BY 10 BY 10 CUBITS
- H.P. = HOLY PLACE—20 BY 10 BY 10 CUBITS
- H. of H. = HOLY OF HOLIES—10 BY 10 BY 10 CUBITS

FURNITURE
1. BRAZEN ALTAR
2. LAVER
3. TABLE OF SHOWBREAD
4. GOLDEN CANDLESTICK
5. ALTAR OF INCENSE
6. ARK OF THE COVENANT

14

THE TABERNACLE OF THE WILDERNESS

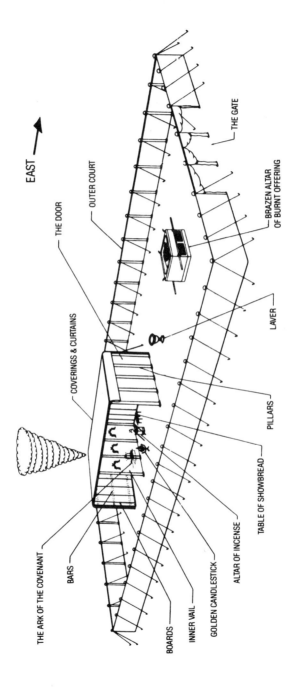

EAST →

THE DOOR

OUTER COURT

THE GATE

BRAZEN ALTAR
OF BURNT OFFERING

LAVER

PILLARS

TABLE OF SHOWBREAD

ALTAR OF INCENSE

COVERINGS & CURTAINS

GOLDEN CANDLESTICK

INNER VAIL

BOARDS

BARS

THE ARK OF THE COVENANT

15

Lesson 2

Leviticus 1:1–7:38

Laws of Offerings

The five offerings described in chapters 1-7 were the five major offerings required of Israelites. Such a large proportion of Leviticus is devoted to the sacrifices and offerings that God required of His people that one must conclude these were a prominent part of Israel's life. And they were. The Tabernacle, or tent of meeting, which in Exodus was a prominent symbol of God's dwelling among His people, would have lost its rich and deep significance without the offerings performed by the priests. Therefore the Lord gave detailed instructions to Moses concerning these services.

Of course the only offerings accepted of God were those made by contrite hearts, obeying in faith the commandments of the Lord. This must be kept in mind as you study these many chapters on the sacrificial system. The offerings were to be the outward expression of the effort of the inward heart to secure and maintain communion with a holy God.

A. Analysis

First read these seven chapters carefully, prayerfully, and repeatedly. It is of utmost importance that you become thoroughly familiar with what the Bible *says* before you try to determine what it *means*. Because of the limitations of space, this manual cannot touch on all aspects of the book of Leviticus. You are encouraged to work much on your own, beyond the suggestions of the manual.

After you have read these chapters a few times, list at least fifteen key words and phrases that are repeated in this section.

_____

_____

_____

You will notice in these seven chapters that only five different offerings are described:
1. The burnt offering, 1:1-17
2. The meal offering (*American Standard Version*), 2:1-16
3. The peace offering, 3:1-17
4. The sin offering, 4:1–5:13
5. The trespass offering, 5:13–6:7

The section 6:8–7:38 gives additional rules concerning these five offerings, especially for the priests' instruction.

When you learn the different purposes of the five offerings, you will be able to appreciate why the sacrificial system became a vital part of Israel's life in Old Testament days. One of the best ways to identify the unique purpose of each offering is to note the similarities and differences. The chart on page 18 shows some of the main items that should be observed.

As you read each representative system of the offerings (e.g. 1:3-9 for burnt offering) record in a word or short phrase whatever applies to that offering opposite the designated subject. For help in determining the main purpose of each offering, consider the following:

1. *Burnt Offering*: Read 6:8-13 and observe the key word here. Notice especially the strong emphasis of verse 13.

2. *Meal Offering*: What is the major difference between this offering and the other four? Fine flour was from the fruit of the soil as well as the result of man's labor. What do these symbols reveal concerning this offering's purpose?

3. *Peace Offering*: Read 7:11-34. This is the only blood sacrifice where the offerer could partake of the flesh. Note also that cakes of several kinds accompanied this offering, suggesting participation in a fellowship meal.

4. *Sin and Trespass Offerings*: Read 7:1-7 and observes the similarity between the two offerings. But there is a noticeable difference. Observe that a prerequisite for the trespass offering is restitution. Note the words "amends" (5:16) and "restore" (6:4-5). The sin offering emphasizes not so much the transgression committed as it does the person sinning and the holy One sinned against. Observe that the blood of the sin offering was sprinkled upon the very horns of the altar (4:7), whereas the blood of the trespass offering was sprinkled in the more general area "round about upon the altar" (7:2).

THE FIVE LEVITICAL OFFERINGS

	BURNT	MEAL	PEACE	SIN	TRESPASS
	1:3-17 6:8-13	2:1-16 6:14-23	3:1-17 7:11-23	4:1—5:13 6:24-30	5:14—6:7 7:1-10
chart represents these passages	1:3-9	2:1-3; 11-13	3:1-5	4:1-12	5:14-16 7:1-5
PRESENTATION					
LAYING ON of HANDS					
KILLING					
SPRINKLING of BLOOD					
BURNING					
OTHER ACTION					
QUALITY of OBJECT SACRIFICED					
MANNER of SACRIFICING					
MAIN PURPOSE of the OFFERING					

Continue your study of the offerings by answering the following:
1. What procedures of offering are common to all five?

_____

_____

_____

2. Which offerings are designated "sweet savour"?

_____

_____

_____

3. What appears to be the significance of laying the hand on the offering?

_____

_____

4. Why would shedding of blood be an important part of the offerings?

_____

_____

5. What spiritual truths are suggested by these phrases:
"made by fire" (1:9)

_____

"sweet savour" (1:9)

_____

"fine flour" (2:1)

_____

"no leaven" (2:11)

_____

"nor . . . honey" (2:11)

_____

"with salt" (2:13)

_____

6. You have probably observed that, for each offering, optional objects are offered (e.g., for the burnt offering: bullock, sheep, or fowl). What was the practical reason behind this?

_____

7. The most important interpretations and applications to be made from these chapters involve the offerings as types of the Person and work of Christ. Read such New Testament passages as Matthew 20:28; Romans 3:24-26; 8:34; 1 Corinthians 15:3; Galatians 1:4; Hebrews 7:25; chapters 9 and 10; 1 Peter 2:24; John 6:51; 17:19; Ephesians 2:11-19.

B. Comments

1. *Primary Teachings of the Offerings.* In order to interpret these offerings we must first discover what God was teaching the Israelites through them. Because scores of symbols and emblems were involved, many practical lessons were taught. We shall list here only some of the major ones:

The Offering	The Israelites
Burnt	Voluntarily devoting all to God, through purifying fire
Meal	Thanking God and offering their lives for His service
Peace	Participating in the blessings of fellowship with God
Sin	Being forgiven because they were sinners
Trespass	Being forgiven for the sins they committed

Now let us identify some of the Christian teachings derived from these Old Testament sacrifices. There are two lines of application: the Christian's offerings and Christ's offerings, shown by the following:

OFFERING			THE CHRISTIAN	CHRIST
BURNT	(SWEET SAVOUR OFFERINGS)	IN COMMUNION WITH GOD	Consecration	He presented Himself to the Father, to do His will.
MEAL			Service	He served His Father and men as Son of Man.
PEACE			Fellowship	He is the common bond of fellowship between God and man.
SIN		FOR COMMUNION WITH GOD	Redemption for the sinner that he is	He atoned for the **guilt** of sin.
TRESPASS			Redemption for the sin that he commits	He atoned for the **damage** of sin.

The story of a person's conversion and spiritual growth may be illustrated by the order in which the offerings are listed here, starting from the bottom (note however that there apparently was a different order when the offerings were actually performed, cf. 9:1-21 and 14:10-20):

(a) *Trespass*. When a man is awakened by the Spirit, the arrow of conviction enters the soul, and his memory casts back its enlightened eye over the page of his past life. He sees it stained with numberless trespasses against God and man and recalls that in the past he has taken God's name in vain, coveted his neighbor's possessions, lied, and repeatedly broken the law of God.

At this point the man is not so much concerned about why or how these trespasses have been committed as he is with the fact that they have been committed and that the penalty for breaking God's law is eternal death. The great question with him now is how to escape this awful penalty. Then the gospel comes and presents Christ in one phase of His work for mankind, the trespass offering, the One through whom all trespasses can be freely forgiven and all damage repaired, because He has already died and paid the penalty for all. The man eagerly accepts Christ and is saved (salvation).

(b) *Sin*. For a while the man rejoices in this phase of Christ's work, thankful that he is saved from the penalty of sin. At first this is all he sees that Christ is able to do for him. Many people never get any further in their apprehension of the work of Christ. But Christ can do much more than save a soul from the penalty of a broken law. He saves not only from the *penalty* but also from the *power* of sin.

The Christian sooner or later begins to see that sins he commits are like branches from a root, or streams from a fountain, and that sin in his nature is the root or fountain. He sees, as did Paul, two laws at war within him. The good he would do he does not, and the evil he would not do he does. Must this struggle go on? How shall he get deliverance from this *power* of sin? In the same way that he got deliverance from the *penalty* of sin—through Christ. (Read Rom. 7:14–8:3.)

He accepts Christ in this phase of His work and has victory. How he rejoices! No longer does that bad temper, that besetting sin, that unholy appetite have dominion. Day by day he can live victoriously over the *power* of sin.

(c) *Peace.* Another ministry of Christ becomes apparent to the Christian by this time. He longs to know more intimately the God who has done so much for him. Is there any way by which he, a weak human creature, can actually commune with the Maker of the universe, talk with Him and know His plans and His will? Yes, through Christ. The gospel presents Christ in this phase of His work, the peace offering. As the peace offering, Christ brings the believer into the very presence of the Father, where there is sweet communion and where he may feed upon Christ as the source of his peace and joy. This is *fellowship.*

(d) *Meal.* Again a deeper work of grace is done in the man's heart. Through this sweet fellowship with God in the peace offering he gets better acquainted with his Lord and begins to see with His eyes and feel with His heart. The great lost world around him begins to touch his heart, and the desire is awakened to live like Christ, who went about doing good, raising the fallen, showing the way of salvation to perishing humanity. He desires not only to be good but to be good for something, to serve as did Christ. The gospel then presents Christ as the meal offering, and as such He is seen in His perfect manhood as He lived and walked and worked down here, the true Pattern for every believer; and the man sees that because of Christ he must present himself for *service.*

(e) *Burnt.* Here the Christian learns something of consecration. He looks back and sees all that has been accomplished in him, his trespasses forgiven, his sin taken away, himself brought into sweet fellowship with his Maker; and now he desires to follow his Master in service. But his desire to *serve* God must be grounded in a deeper yearning to *glorify* God in every aspect of his living. He wishes to live for the glory of God. That is consecration. The gospel presents Christ as the burnt offering, the only One who can enable a believer to live this life of entire consecration, where all is for the glory of God. Not primarily for the good of humanity does he live and serve now, but that God may be glorified by his life and service.

* * *

The order in which we have been considering the offerings above gives us man's view of Christ's work, a gradually widening view. But when we begin at the top of the list with the burnt offering and go downward, we get God's view of Christ's work.

The first view God has of His matchless Son is the burnt offering view, that of full consecration. Christ, before He came to earth, presented Himself without spot to God, ready to do His Father's will, whatever that might be.

In the *meal offering* God sees His only begotten Son with His glory laid aside. He has come down to earth, has taken upon Him the form of man, and is walking and working among men, preaching the gospel, healing the sick, raising the dead, living the life of service.

Next God sees Him in the *peace offering* aspect. Some to whom He has preached have believed. They are living and walking and working with Him and seeing God in Him. They are getting acquainted with God's power and mercy and love and wisdom as they see these things in Christ. They are actually enjoying fellowship with God through Him.

In the *sin offering* God sees His Son in combat with Satan: in Gethsemane, on the cross, meeting and fighting and conquering the enemy, and then by His death paying man's debt of sin.

And in the *trespass offering* Christ's death is seen to meet the need of every individual sinner, satisfying the claims for every transgression of the law.

God in His grace sent Christ to shed His blood for the sins of all people—people who lived before His time, in His time, and all future generations. It is this blood alone that takes away sin—the blood of bulls and goats could never do this (Heb. 10:4-10). What then was the occasion and purpose of the Levitical offerings? They were part of the Old Testament gospel (1) *informing* men of their lost condition and (2) *inviting* them to believe in the Lord and obey His Word, receiving salvation. Understanding of any prophetic purposes of the offerings was *not* a requisite for salvation. But *faith* was the requirement, as it still is. "By grace are ye saved through faith" (Eph. 2:8).

2. *Other Symbolic Teachings.* Before leaving your study of these offerings, spend a little time with some other prominent symbols of the rituals. Some suggestions are made below.

23

(a) *Burnt offering.* That spotless male was skinned, cut in pieces (thus seen to be inwardly as well as outwardly without blemish), *all* burned on the altar ("the table of the Lord")—the head, the fat, the legs, the inwards, every part given to God. This offering most beautifully sets forth the spotless Christ, absolutely without internal or external blemish, surrendering every part of His being wholly to God, and enabling the believer to live this life of full consecration.

(b) *Meal offering.* Observe how accurately this pictures Christ's life on earth. The flour (earthly fruit) speaks of His humanity; the *fine* flour speaks of the perfect character of this humanity. The oil (symbol of the Spirit), mingled with and poured upon the flour, indicates the action of the Holy Spirit in His conception and at His baptism. Honey (earthly sweets) and leaven (type of sin) were excluded, as all sin and merely earthly pleasure were excluded from Christ's life, but salt (purifying and preserving) was always included.

(c) *Peace offering.* Here we see Christ enjoyed by the believer in communion with God, both the believer and God having their share in Christ. Notice God's part: the fat (inner excellencies), kidneys (hidden energies), caul (tender sensibilities). These are the parts of Christ that God could enjoy. Man's part of the peace offering is just what he needs and can appreciate: the shoulder (strength) and the breast (love).

(d) *Sin and trespass offerings.* Neither of these offerings was a sweet savor to God, for sin is not sweet to God. These offerings clearly foreshadowed the details of Christ's atoning work: the victim without spot or blemish; transfer of the sins of the offerer to the offering by laying on of hands; the offering dying in the sinner's place; the blood presented before God; the (sin) offering carried without the camp.

C. Summary

The study of the Levitical offerings is not an easy lesson. But the truths taught in this book of the Bible are of great importance to us because they serve to emphasize in a vivid, concrete way the crucial facts of spiritual life and death. As you summarize the contents of Leviticus 1–7, list the *big* truths taught about:
Who God is

What sin is

_____

_____

What sin brings

_____

_____

How a man is saved

_____

_____

Christ, the key of the offerings

_____

_____

In light of these offerings, how much have you appropriated of Christ?

Laws of Consecration of the Priests

At this point the Israelites had the Tabernacle and its furniture as well as instructions concerning the required offerings. (See Ex. 25–40; Lev. 1–7.) Now they needed a functioning priesthood to minister to them in these rituals of worship, as God had indicated earlier (Ex. 28–29). The three chapters studied in this lesson record the story of the consecration of the priest Aaron and his four sons: Nadab, Abihu, Eleazar, and Ithamar. The inauguration of the priestly ministry began a new era in Israel's career, when God, through clear and unmistakable signs, symbols, and events, showed forth daily His righteousness, grace, and glory.

I. CONSECRATION OF THE PRIESTS (8:1–9:24)

A. Analysis

First read Exodus 28 and 29 as background for this section. (The detailed coverage of these chapters explains why Moses can be so brief in Lev. 8:1-5.) Also read chapters 5 and 7–9 of Hebrews, observing that while Christ is the antitype of Aaron the high priest, He is also the *incomparable* high priest, who offered up Himself once and for all for the sins of all mankind (Heb. 7:27).

Now read these chapters of Leviticus two or three times, watching carefully as the story alternates between *instruction* and *action*. Here are some suggestions for your study:

1. As you read, underline key words and phrases, such as "sanctify" and "consecrate."

2. Concerning things said or done, note especially the parts played by the Lord, Moses, Aaron, and the sons of Aaron.

3. In order to help you see the main structure of these chapters, study the schematic chart on page 28.

4. Observe from the chart that there are two large and two small segments in this section. If necessary read the two chapters of Leviticus again to justify this outline.
5. Read 8:1-5. Jot down in the appropriate place on the chart a few key items of this paragraph. What is the people's interest in this ceremony?

From whom did Aaron receive his call to this ministry? (Read Heb. 5:4)

---

6. Moses is the main actor in 8:6-30. What are the prominent things he does in consecrating the priests and Tabernacle? List them briefly in the three paragraphs on the chart. What spiritual truths underlie the main items of the consecration referred to in 8:6-9?

Concerning the significance of washing, read Isaiah 4:4; John 3:5; 15:3; Titus 3:5. Notice in Exodus 28:2 that the holy garments were "for glory and for beauty." On what parts of the body was the blood of consecration applied?

What is the significance?

Note how Aaron is distinguished from his sons. Keep in mind that Aaron as high priest was a type of Christ (Heb. 5:4-5; 7:11), and his sons types of believers (1 Peter 2:5, 9).
7. Read 8:31-36. Like 8:1-5, this is a paragraph consisting mainly of instruction. But note verse 36. What is the time duration of this paragraph?

What significance would the Israelites *see* in the number *seven*?

LEVITICUS 8-9   READ EXODUS 28-29

8:1 MAINLY INSTRUCTION	8:6 MAINLY ACTION	8:31 MAINLY INSTRUCTION	9:1 MAINLY ACTION
INTRODUCTION	MOSES CONSECRATES AARON AND SONS	7 DAYS' CONSECRATION	AARON BEGINS TO SERVE
8:1 "LORD SPAKE UNTO MOSES"	6 MOSES—MAIN ACTOR	8:31 "MOSES SAID UNTO AARON AND TO HIS SONS. . . ."	1 AARON—MAIN ACTOR
8:5 "MOSES DID AS THE LORD COMMANDED HIM"	10	8:36 "AARON AND HIS SONS DID. . . ."	8
	14		22
	30		24

28

8. Segment 9:1-24 records the first duties performed by Aaron as a consecrated high priest. Record on the chart key items of the segment. Observe the appearances of the phrase "glory of the Lord." What other things happened on this momentous day, according to 9:22-24?

_____

_____

_____

What was God teaching in all of this?

_____

_____

9. A summary question: List various spiritual lessons that you think the Israelites could have learned from this inspiring ceremony of the consecration of their priests.

_____

_____

_____

10. What types of Christ's priestly ministry do you see in these chapters?

_____

_____

11. Since all Christians are priests of God, what are the many vital spiritual lessons that Christians may learn and apply from these chapters? List at least ten of these.

_____

_____

_____

_____

_____

_____

29

B. Comments

Consecration means "set apart" for God. A wholly separated, consecrated person or thing is simply one set apart for God and God's service. God had previously chosen Aaron and his sons to minister in the Tabernacle (Ex. 28), but these chapters describe the actual ceremony of their consecration.

This ceremony was important and impressive. From 8:1-5 we note that all Israel, at the command of God, had assembled at the door of the Tabernacle to see Aaron and his sons robed and anointed for their offices. Naturally the people would be much interested. Aaron was to be their high priest, the one who would represent them before God and bring His messages to them. He was to be the medium of communication between Jehovah and themselves. Each article of Aaron's dress was intended to set forth some special qualification of the high priest, and it may be that as each garment was put on in the presence of the people, Moses explained something of its significance. Aaron, in his office of high priest, occupied for Israel the place Christ now occupies for the church. Christ is our High Priest, the One who represents us before God and who communicates God's will to us. In Christ we see the realities of which these garments of Aaron were only the shadow. Let us study these now:

1. The first garment placed upon Aaron was the pure white *linen coat*. From this we learn that the first qualification of the high priest is purity. The absolute purity of our great High Priest is evident to men and angels.

2. Next came the *girdle*, which was the symbol of service. Although Aaron held a most exalted position in the camp, yet he was the servant of Israel, constantly ministering in their behalf, doing them the greatest possible service. So Christ, "although He existed in the form of God, did not regard equality with God a thing to be grasped, but emptied Himself, taking the form of a bondservant" (Phil. 2:6-7, *New American Standard Bible*); and now He is at the Father's right hand constantly ministering in our behalf.

3. Then Moses clothed Aaron with the *robe of the ephod*, that long garment of blue, the color of heaven, suggesting the heavenly origin of the priesthood. Aaron had not been elected by man to this office but had been appointed by God. So Christ was appointed by God to be our High Priest (Heb. 5:4-6).

4. Over the robe of the ephod was placed the *ephod*, which was distinctively the high priest's garment. There would be many priests, but there could be only one high priest, only one who could represent the people before God or go into the Holy of Holies and make atonement for them; this garment was worn only by

the one who held that office. Likewise there are many believers today, but there can be but one High Priest, only One who can represent us before God and make atonement for us.

5. You will notice in the description of the ephod (Ex. 28:6-14), that the front and back pieces were joined at the shoulder by two onyx stones on which were engraved the names of the tribes of Israel. And in the breastplate, that square piece of linen that was placed on the ephod upon Aaron's breast, twelve precious stones were set, and upon each one was engraved the name of a tribe. So when Aaron represented the people before God, he bore the name of every tribe upon his strong shoulders and his loving breast, just as our great High Priest bears us all before God. His strength and His love are both exercised in behalf of every believing child, just as we saw that in the peace offering the breast and the shoulder were man's portion.

6. Last, there was placed upon Aaron's head the *mitre* with its band of gold on which was written, "Holiness to the Lord" (Ex. 28:36-38). Read carefully verse 38 and notice that, because of this holiness seen upon Aaron, the people were accepted before the Lord. How true all this is of our High Priest, Jesus. The mitre had a kingly as well as a priestly import, indicating that Aaron had authority in the camp and that his voice must be obeyed. Similarly Christ is King as well as Priest.

* * *

After Aaron had been robed, Moses anointed both the Tabernacle and the priests with oil. In the Scriptures oil is consistently a symbol of the Holy Spirit. The anointing of the Holy Spirit is a prerequisite for service to God, as shown in the experience of Jesus at the beginning of His public ministry. (Read Luke 3:22; 4:18; Acts 10:38.)

A special offering made at this consecration service was that of the "ram of consecration" (8:22-29). Observe that Moses put blood on the right ears, on the thumbs of the right hands, and on the big toes of the right feet of Aaron and his sons. The meaning of this is plain. Their ears now were consecrated to God, and amid all the voices round about they must be listening only for God's voice. Their hands now were consecrated to the service of God, and their feet were to walk the holy courts of the Lord's house. We also, as priests unto God, should have the consecrated ear, hand, and foot, and be constantly listening for His voice, doing His work, and walking in the path in which He leads.

After the consecration services, the first thing Aaron and his sons did was to make the offerings as directed in chapters 1–7

(Lev. 9:1-5). As the offering lay upon the altar, see the startling thing that occurred (9:24). No wonder the people shouted and fell on their faces as they saw how God accepted the sacrifice. This was holy fire and had to be kept burning. No other was to be used in the service of the Tabernacle (see Lev. 16:12).

II. DEFILEMENT (10:1-20)

A. Analysis

This is the chapter of (1) "strange fire," an offering made contrary to the commandment of God, and (2) the sequel of another irregular offering. After you have read the chapter twice, record your observations of key words and phrases on the accompanying chart (p. 33). Then follow these suggestions for study:

1. How is this chapter related to the two preceding ones?

_____

_____

2. Compare 10:1 with Exodus 30:9.

_____

_____

3. Compare the fires of these four verses: 9:24; 10;1; 10:2; 10:16.

_____

_____

_____

4. How did Moses interpret the judgment of God? (10:3).

_____

5. Why were Aaron and his sons forbidden to mourn for the death of their loved ones?

_____

_____

According to verses 6 and 7, how were obligations to family and ministry differentiated?

_____

_____

32

LEVITICUS 10

STRANGE FIRE	EVENT	1	Try to determine the main contribution of each paragraph to the story of the chapter.
	DISPOSITION	3	
	REGULATIONS	8	↑ How is this paragraph related to what goes before?
UNEATEN SACRIFICE		12	How is this related to the next paragraph? ↓
	EVENT	16	
	DISPOSITION	19 20	

33

6. Compare the sin of Nadab and Abihu with that of Eleazar and Ithamar (vv. 16-18).

One what basis did Moses accept Aaron's explanation?

7. What spiritual lessons do you learn from this chapter?

B. Comments

In this chapter we are told how two of Aaron's sons violated God's law and were instantly struck dead (10:1-2). This was no light offense but flagrant disobedience and presumption. They had dared to do what the Lord had forbidden them to do. The strange fire that they offered apparently had not been taken from the brazen altar. It would seem from verse 1 that Nadab and Abihu not only offered strange fire but also went into the Holy of Holies (see Lev. 16:12), performing an office that belonged only to Aaron, the high priest. So their offense was that they burned incense to God with fire not taken from the altar, and they themselves went into the presence of God, not recognizing the office of the high priest. Basically the sin of Aaron's sons was disobedience to God, and the judgment for such sin should be ample warning to Christians —priests of God today.

The death of Aaron's two sons must have been a heavy blow to their father, but notice how he received it: "And Aaron held his peace." He recognized the hand of God and knew all was well. This offense had been committed at a critical time in the history of the people; it was as if God deemed it necessary thus to show His displeasure in order to impress the lesson on the nation.

Aaron and his surviving sons were not allowed to mourn for their dead (10:6-7). They led the worship of the congregation, and that had to go on uninterrupted. It was of far more importance than any private bereavement.

In order to grasp the meaning of 10:12-20, as well as to understand the displeasure of Moses and why he was "content" with Aaron's excuse, it will be necessary to read Leviticus 6:24-30 and to remember that this eating of the sin offering was the most elevated form of priestly service since it exhibited God's gracious acceptance of the sacrifice. Apparently Aaron's sons, subdued in spirit over their brothers' deaths, were not able to rise to such high ground, and they would not pretend to a spiritual power that they did not possess. If anything, they wanted to be sure their heart attitude was one of humility and contriteness, as they felt unworthy of God's favor. Aaron their father felt the same way, and Moses was satisfied with the explanation.

III. SUMMARY

From these chapters at least four prominent truths concerning the priests strike the reader:

1. The *source* of their ministry: Chosen of God
2. The *consecration* of their ministry: Equipped by God
3. The *functions* of their ministry: Offering to God
4. A *warning* about their ministry: Disobeying commandments of God

See how much of the narrative you can recall to illustrate these four subjects.

Lesson 4

Leviticus 11:1–15:33

Laws of Purity

Before reading these chapters, it is well to review the large structural outline of Leviticus 1–17 by recalling this part of the chart given earlier:

LEVITICUS 1-17

1	8	11	16 17
LAWS of OFFERINGS	LAWS of CONSECRATION of PRIESTS	LAWS of PURITY	DAY of ATONEMENT
THE WAY TO GOD			

If God was impressing one truth on the hearts of the Israelites concerning the *way* to fellowship with Him, it was this: "Ye shall be holy for I am holy." The sound of such words must have echoed in the Israelites' ears over and over again, whether by way of the laws of offerings, the laws of consecration of the priests, the laws of purity, or the instructions concerning the day of atonement. And they must have seen in all of these God's provision to make them holy and acceptable to Him. Keep that always in mind as you interpret the chapters of this lesson.

36

A. Analysis

The instructions regarding the Tabernacle services and the priests having been given, God now teaches the people as to the purity that will be expected on their part. He tells them that they must be clean in regard to two things: food (11), and diseases and issues (12–15).

1. First read through the chapters in one sitting. Your reaction to reading these chapters (and others like them in Leviticus) will probably be the common and understandable one: the content is difficult, repetitious, and appears to be remote from Christian living today. Do not let this detract you. Someone has well said, "The laws have all passed away, but the principles they embodied are still burning and practical." In our study we are especially searching for these principles.

2. Underline key words and phrases as you read and circle any verses or groups of verses that teach timeless, universal truths.

3. Make a list of eight or ten observations from this reading.

_____

_____

_____

_____

_____

_____

4. Record on the accompanying chart the key items of each paragraph or segment. Do not attempt to be exhaustive as to the many details. By so condensing this section of Leviticus, you will be in a better position to see the prominent things.

5. "Clean" and "unclean" are obviously two key words of this passage ("unclean" appears more than 100 times). Were the laws of difference purely arbitrary?

_____

Were they given to help the Israelites physically?

_____

If so, how?

_____

_____

_____

LAWS OF PURITY
LEVITICUS 11-15

"Make a difference between the unclean and the clean" 11:47			
11:1	12:1	13:1	15:1
ANIMALS	CHILDBIRTH	LEPROSY	ISSUES
11:1 **DIET**	12:1 MAN CHILD	13:1 **RECOGNIZING LEPROSY**	15:1 **MAN**
		13:47 **LEPROSY IN GARMENTS**	
	12:5 MAID CHILD		
11:24 PHYSICAL CONTACT		14:1 **CLEANSING THE LEPER**	15:19 **WOMAN**
	12:6 EITHER		
		14:33 **LEPROSY IN HOUSES**	

38

Did God intend to teach spiritual truths by these laws of purity?

_____

_____

If so, identify some. (Read James 4:4-8.)

_____

_____

_____

6. Is God less concerned about the health of Christians today than He was about the Israelites' health? How important is a person's body in the sight of God?

_____

_____

How is one's soul related to the body?

_____

_____

What does the New Testament teach about the Christian's body? (Use a concordance to help you here.)

_____

_____

_____

7. Did the uncleanness of a mother after childbirth (chap. 12) teach any spiritual truth to the Israelites? If so, what?

_____

_____

_____

8. The uncleannesses of chapter 11 were avoidable, whereas most of the uncleannesses of chapters 12–15 were unavoidable. How is the spiritual nature of man illustrated by this?

_____

_____

_____

9. Why was leprosy banished so promptly from the camp of Israel?

_____

10. In what three ways is leprosy a type of sin?

_____

_____

11. Why did the priest take extreme precaution in diagnosing leprosy accurately?

_____

What spiritual lesson may be learned from this?

_____

12. Why was there a cleansing of the leper *after* the healing had taken place?

_____

13. The laws of living that God gave the Israelites for their life in Canaan made them a people different from their neighbors. But was the difference intended to be basically over *what they did* or over *whom they served*? (Study 11:44-45 carefully before answering.)

_____

How is this principle applied in Christian living?

_____

_____

B. Comments

1. *First.* Note what God says regarding clean and unclean food (chap. 11).

Down in Egypt the Israelites apparently had eaten without pattern or scruples; but after they were brought into association with the holy God they had to observe the differences between clean and unclean things even in the matter of food, as these differences were taught of God. (Cf. Acts 10:9-16.)

The clean beasts were all those that chewed the cud and parted the hoof (vv. 1-8). Both marks were necessary; one was not sufficient. The animals forbidden were those especially liable to parasitic diseases. It is interesting to observe that the meat diet of the Israelites was restricted largely to the domestic animals used in

40

sacrifice. And God's choices of the sacrificial animals were not arbitrary.

God considered those fish to be clean that had fins and scales. Since fins were for motion and scales for resistance, one may see in this an illustration of two necessary Christian qualities: an ever progressing witness and resistance to all evil hindrances. Among the birds (vv. 13-47), all those that fed on flesh, those that ate everything promiscuously, and those that groveled on the ground, although furnished with wings to soar into heaven, were pronounced unclean. We can easily make the application.

2. *Second.* Note what God says about uncleanness as to diseases and issues (chaps. 12–15).

(a) *Uncleanness of the mother after childbirth.* "The only adequate explanation of the seeming anomaly presented by the command to be fruitful, the joy attending the realization of parenthood, and the uncleanness that is associated with it . . . must be found in the fact of the fall and the curse pronounced on woman immediately after it. . . . From this it follows that, although the birth of a child is a joyous event, it is also a solemn one. For the birth of the child will inevitably be followed ultimately by its death, and by eternal death unless the child is made an heir of life through the redemption that is in Christ."[1]

(b) *Leprosy.* The Hebrew word is *tsara'ath* (from a root meaning "scourge") and may possibly describe different kinds of skin diseases (13:1-46; 14:1-32) and fungus conditions (13:47-59; 14:33-53). The prominent symptoms (e.g., numbness) of present-day leprosy are noticeably absent from the account, and for this and other reasons many Bible scholars and medical experts believe *tsara'ath* is not the common leprosy, or Hansen's Disease, known today. Whatever the case, the similarities as to causes, types, diagnostic care, infection, loathsomeness, disposition, and curability are strong enough to warrant retaining the word "leprosy" in the studies of these chapters. The underlying purpose of the laws concerning *tsara'ath* was to impress upon the Israelites the spiritual truths taught thereby.

Leprosy typifies sin in various ways. For example: (1) it is loathsome, (2) it spreads easily where care is not taken, and (3) it leaves scars and marks. God said leprosy was a thing that should not be allowed in the congregation of Israel, and the utmost diligence was to be exercised to keep free of it. When it was found in a garment, the garment had to be burned. When it appeared in a house, the house was to be torn down; and when it appeared in a

1. F. Davidson et al., eds., *The New Bible Commentary* (Grand Rapids: Eerdmans, 1953), pp. 145-46.

person, the person was banished from the camp. D. L. Leiker, a leading expert on leprosy treatment, says: "Frequent bathing, washing of clothes, and keeping a clean house will help to prevent the disease, because many bacilli can be washed away with water and soap before they enter the skin. The most important thing is to avoid bodily contact with infectious cases of leprosy."[2]

Observe the great care that was shown in order to ascertain whether a disease was really leprosy, before taking action. A careful and deliberate examination was made. Washing the garment, removing stones from the house, and other procedures were followed in efforts to correct the trouble without resorting to banishment. But when a disease was found to be really leprosy, then unsparing measures were applied in obedience to God's command and for the health of the camp.

Thinking of leprosy as a type of sin, can we not learn some important lessons? First, sin should not be harbored in the church of Christ, and the utmost diligence should be exercised to keep it from its destructive course. The reason leprosy and all uncleanness was to be promptly banished from the camp of Israel was because the holy God dwelt in their midst. That is the chief reason that sin and uncleanness should not be tolerated. "Know ye not that your body is the temple of the Holy Ghost that is in you?" (1 Cor. 6:19). When such a Person condescends to be our Guest, He should have a clean place in which to dwell. Read what 2 Corinthians 6:14-18 has to say about separation.

Second, if not dealt with adequately, sin keeps growing to larger proportions, begetting other sins. Dr. Leiker in the same article describes the spreading character of infectious leprosy thus: "The germs multiply and spread through the blood to all parts of the body. At first the disease cannot be seen, but gradually large areas of the skin become thickened. First signs of the disease are usually seen on the face."[3]

A third lesson to be learned from these chapters is that things that may look like sin should not be condemned without proper investigation. There once lived a man who was a drunkard before becoming a Christian. A few months after his conversion he was frequently seen to enter saloons. This was reported to the local church, and the man was brought before the congregation to answer to the charge. Only then was it found that he had been preaching the gospel to his old associates. There had not been proper investigation before pronouncing his activities as sin.

2. *Africa Now*, XXII, 1964.
3. Ibid.

Let us not overlook the bright side of the lesson to be learned from these chapters, namely, that there is a cleansing for sin. The ceremony by which a healed leper was declared clean and allowed back into the camp (14:1-20) is a beautiful picture of the way in which a sinner is cleansed and restored. One of two birds was killed in an earthen vessel, as Christ the heavenly One died in an earthly vessel (His body), and His blood was given to cleanse us from all sin (1 John 1:7). A living bird was let "loose into the open field," symbolizing the restoration of the believer who had sinned to the fellowship of Christ and His people.

(c) *Issues*. Chapter 15 tells of various uncleannesses of issues from the physical organs. The lessons of this chapter are related to those of chapter 12. "Wash" is the important part of the ceremony in the cleansing from issues, though it is to be observed that blood sacrifices were also a requirement.

C. Summary

Keeping in mind the principles underlying the standards by which God distinguished between clean and unclean things, write out contrasting lists of sinful and righteous activities in the following areas of present-day living:

SINFUL ACTIVITIES	AREA	RIGHTEOUS ACTIVITIES
	HEALTH HABITS	
	AMUSEMENTS	
	READING	
	COMPANIONS	
	BUSINESS	
	GOALS	

Lesson 5

Laws of the Day of Atonement

The Day of Atonement was the most important day of Israel's calendar, for then the idea of atonement for sin reached its high-
est expression. Only on this day could the high priest enter into
the Most Holy Place of the Tabernacle. This was the only day of the
year for which fasting was required, in bold contrast to the atmosphere of rejoicing that attended the annual feasts. On no other
day were the Israelites more strongly impressed with the *grace* of
God in forgiving all their sins. The gospel of this day was a bright
sign of the coming gospel of the Lord Jesus Christ.

I. THE DAY OF ATONEMENT (16:1-34)

A. Analysis

First read through chapter 16, making a mental note of your impressions as well as underlining key phrases in your Bible. As you
read this chapter a second time paragraph by paragraph, observe
the procedures of the day's ceremonies. Be able to explain why
some of the same items are referred to more than once. Study the
accompanying outline. Observe the appearances of each item in
the boxes shown. Use the chart also to record any other items that
seem important.

Now continue in your study by following these suggestions:
1. Notice how all-inclusive this offering was (vv. 30, 34). Did this
annual offering, made by the high priest, make the daily offerings
of the people obsolete?

_____

_____

_____

45

DAY of ATONEMENT
LEVITICUS 16

PARAGRAPH	OUTLINE		ATONEMENT for AARON AND HIS HOUSE	AARON'S GARMENTS	ATONEMENT for the PEOPLE	ATONEMENT for TABERNACLE
1-5	INTRO					
6-10	GENERAL PROCEDURE		bullock —sin offering ▶×	linen garments put on	2 goats —sin offering ▶×	
11-14	for AARON and HIS HOUSE	DETAILED PROCEDURE	ram —burnt offering ▶×			
15-19	for PEOPLE and TABERNACLE	DETAILED PROCEDURE			slain goat ▶	holy place —altar
20-22	for PEOPLE and TABERNACLE	DETAILED PROCEDURE			scape-goat ▶	
23-28	CONCLUDING CEREMONIES		▶×	linen garments exchanged	ram —burnt offering ▶×	
29-34	FINAL INSTRUCTIONS and SUMMARY					

46

What do you think was the relationship between the two?

_____

2. What truths about atonement for sin are typified in the ceremonies over the slain goat and the scapegoat? (Read Ps. 103:12;
Isa. 38:17; 43:25; Jer. 31:34; Mic. 7:19; John 1:29; Heb. 9:26.)

_____

_____

_____

3. What spiritual truths are taught by the linen garments of the
high priest?

_____

the required atonement for the Tabernacle and its furniture?

_____

and the restricted permission to enter the Most Holy Place only
once a year?

_____

What do you see of *God's grace* in the very fact of a high priestly
ministry?

_____

_____

4. Read Hebrews 9:7-28. List the various ways the sacrifices of the
Day of Atonement typified Christ's atoning work.

_____

_____

_____

_____

47

B. Comments

The root meaning of our English word *atonement* is "at-one-ment," that is, the bringing together of two parties who have been at enmity into a relationship of peace and fellowship. The following description of *atonement* is quoted from Arthur B. Fowler:

"The word belongs primarily to the Old Testament, as it occurs only once in the New Testament (Rom. 5:11) and there the ASV properly renders it 'reconciliation.'

"The words 'atonement,' 'make atonement,' 'appease,' 'pacify,' etc., from the Hebrew root *kaphar* occur about one hundred and ten times in the Old Testament, principally in Leviticus and Numbers, and the root idea is 'to cover.' The primitive verb and its noun occur in Genesis 6:14, '*pitch* it within and without with pitch.' Just as the pitch covered the ark and protected its inmates, so the shed blood of sacrifices stands between man and the outraged law of a holy God. . . .

"The beautiful word 'mercy-seat' for the covering of the ark of the covenant comes from the same word, and has been rendered by some as just 'covering,' but the beauty of the meaning is thus lost. The sprinkling of the blood upon the mercy-seat (Lev. 16:14) was the divine way of picturing the merciful covering of our sins."[1]

Here in Leviticus 16 the doctrine of atonement is set forth as though God would show us by one grand object lesson the many aspects of this sublime truth. It will help us to observe carefully the ceremonies of this important day. Refer to the diagram of the Tabernacle on page 14 to help you visualize the action.

We observe from the text that the high priest's dress is different from that worn on ordinary days. He laid aside the robes for "glory and beauty" about which we read in a previous lesson and was now clothed only in white linen (16:4). Of course, in presenting the sin offering for himself (which was necessary because he himself was but a man—see Heb. 5:1-3), Aaron is not a type of Christ; but in all his work for the *congregation* on the Day of Atonement he is seen as a type of Christ accomplishing the work of atonement.

Two goats were taken from the people for this particular sin offering, because two sides of atonement were to be represented—the Godward and the manward side. At the door of the Tabernacle, Aaron cast lots upon them. This lot determined which goat was to be given to the Lord in sacrifice and which was to be

---

1. M. C. Tenney, ed., "Atonement," *The Zondervan Pictorial Bible Dictionary* (Grand Rapids: Zondervan, 1963) pp. 83-84.

the scapegoat to be driven into the wilderness. But before making the sin offering for the people, or presenting the blood of the sin offering for himself, Aaron took the censer of coals from the altar, and handfuls of incense, causing a fragant smoke in the Holy of Holies to cover the Mercy Seat, so that he might not look directly upon the Shekinah fire and die (16:12-13; cf. Ex. 33:20).

Then he was ready to begin the real work of the day. One goat was slain and its blood brought in and presented to God. Next Aaron took the live goat, laid his hands on its head, and confessed over it all the sins of the people; and this goat, bearing the sins of the people, was led away into the wilderness, a land not inhabited (vv. 20-22).

What does this mean? One goat was killed and its blood presented to God; the other goat was sent away bearing the sins of the people. We see here pictured before us the two sides of atonement—one showing what atonement did in relation to God, and the other what it did for man. Christ's atonement met all the *claims* of God and all the *needs* of man. The claims of God were met by the death of Christ in place of the sinner; and the needs of man were met in taking away his sins, removing them "as far as the east is from the west." As we look at the goat that was slain, we see Christ dying in our place, paying the penalty for sin and thus satisfying the claims of God's holy law—bringing to our mind such passages as Isaiah 53:5, Romans 4:25, Hebrews 9:28, and 1 Peter 2:24. But when we look at the scapegoat, laden down with the sins of Israel and bearing them away into a land not inhabited, we see what happened to our sins, and call to mind such passages as John 1:29, Psalm 103:12, Romans 8:1, and Isaiah 43:25.

Before leaving this chapter, let us tabulate some of the likenesses of Christ's and Aaron's high priestly ministries:

Israel's high priest (Lev. 16)	Our High Priest (Heb. 9)
(1) Aaron, called of God from among men	(1) Christ, called of God from among men (Heb. 5:4, 10)
(2) Had compassion for the wayward (Heb. 5:2)	(2) Prayed with tears (Heb. 5:7)
(3) In spotless purity of dress	(3) In spotless purity of character
(4) Entered the Holy of Holies	(4) Entered heaven itself (Heb. 9:24)
(5) Made complete atonement (by offering the blood of a goat)	(5) Made complete atonment (by offering His own blood)
(6) For the whole nation (Israel) **and** for himself	(6) For the whole human race (John 3:16); **not** for Himself
(7) Offered continually, from year to year	(7) Offered once, for all eternity (Heb. 9:25)

II. THE SIGNIFICANCE OF SACRIFICE (17:1-16)

Chapter 17 is a fitting supplement to chapter 16, for it emphasizes two of the major aspects of sacrifice, namely, the undivided *loyalty* of sacrifice and the key *substance* of sacrifice.

After reading through the chapter once or twice, come back to it with the view to seeing these two major truths emphasized:
1. The undivided loyalty of sacrifice (17:1-9). Observe how important it was that sacrifices should be brought "unto the Lord" (v. 5) and not "unto devils, after whom they have gone a whoring" (v. 7).
2. The key substance of sacrifice (vv. 10-16). Verse 11 is the strategic verse here. Why was *nothing less* than blood accepted by God for atonement?

_____

_____

_____

Arthur M. Barnett, medical missionary of the Africa Inland Mission, once related this experience:

"The sterile quiet of Hackensack Hospital was suddenly disrupted on the Fourth of July by a literal flood of patients pouring in on ambulances, trucks, and cars—the result of a tragedy in a nearby town. A car at an auto-racing arena had suddenly left the track and gone ploughing into the crowd of spectators, creating panic and death and sending this stream of groaning victims to the door.

"I was called immediately to the emergency room. Several other doctors were there as well. We disregarded for the moment a score of less serious injured ones and pitted all our skill and strength against the breathless march of death on those whose wounds were most severe.

"Several were wheeled into the operating room together. We looked at the small boy. It was too late for him. He died before our eyes. We turned to the dead boy's father. Both his legs were mangled. He was dying even then from loss of blood. But we would not give him up. Feverishly we worked. A donor of blood was found in haste. We placed him on a stretcher close by the side of the dying man. An arm of each was bared and scrubbed and sterilized. I plunged a needle into the donor's arm and drew out a syringe full of rich red blood, handed it to my superior, and attached a new syringe to the needle in the vein for more. The other doctor injected the life-giving fluid into the patient's vein, syringe by syringe, watching him closely all the while. Slowly the tide seemed to turn. And then we knew he had a chance to live. Exultation was ours. We had foiled the dark dread enemy of man and saved a soul from death. Through this transfusion and others that followed, in combination with several operations and months of patient nursing, this one as good as dead was restored once more to health and usefulness.

"A week or two after this incident, at a summer Bible conference, I found myself sitting at the Lord's Table, thinking of the wine representing the blood of the Lord Jesus Christ and the bread representing His body. Suddenly it occurred to me that the blood of Christ shed on the cross of Calvary constituted the greatest blood transfusion this world has ever known. As I reflected on the subject that morning, and as I have meditated on it since that time, I have had an increased understanding of the power in that blood.

"The person of the Lord Jesus Christ is the greatest subject of the Bible. His person gives value to His shed blood. This blood is the very life of Christian faith just as the blood is the *sine qua non* of medicine. Take the blood from the body, and you have nothing left but a corpse. Take the blood of Calvary from Christianity, and you have lifeless creed instead of living faith."[2]

> "For the life of the flesh is in the blood: and I have given it to you upon the altar to make an atonement for your souls: for it is the blood that maketh an atonement for the soul." (Lev. 17:11)

SUMMARY

Summarize the prominent teachings of these two chapters by relating them to who God is in His
Holiness

_____

_____

Justice

_____

_____

Grace

_____

_____

2. Arthur M. Barnett, "Life . . . in the Blood" (New York: Africa Inland Mission, n.d.).

List all the prominent truths involved in the doctrine of atonement that you have learned from your study of Leviticus 16 and 17.

_____

_____

_____

_____

_____

_____

_____

Lesson 6
Leviticus 18:1–22:33

Holy People
and Holy Priests

With this lesson we begin our study of the latter half of Leviticus, which is called "The Walk with God." Beginning at chapter 18 God instructs the Israelites through Moses concerning their walk with Him, in anticipation of their settling down in the permanent homeland of Canaan. The Israelites had come out of a land where the personal habits of the native dwellers were vile and wicked in the extreme; and they were going into a land where the inhabitants practiced even worse things. But God, at Sinai, formulated a new code of laws to govern the behavior of His people (chaps. 18–22). Because the Israelites were His people and He was their God, they were to keep His statutes and His ordinances, regardless of the behavior of other nations. Read 18:1-5, observing the personal pronouns and the verbs of "doing."

As we enter this latter half of Leviticus, let us review the outline given earlier:

LEVITICUS 18-27

18	21	23	26	27
HOLY PEOPLE	HOLY PRIESTS	HOLY TIMES	JUST RECOMPENSE	HOLY VOWS
THE WALK WITH GOD				

Recall the key verse of Leviticus: "Ye shall be holy: for I the Lord your God am holy" (19:2*b*). Chapters 1–17 spoke of the holy *way* to God, through atonement by an acceptable substitutionary sacrifice. Now Leviticus begins to discuss the holy *walk* with God, and it is from this vantage point that we will view the chapters.

EXODUS 20 TEN COMMANDMENTS	LEVITICUS 19 LAWS FOR HOLY PEOPLE
I I am the Lord thy God, which have brought thee out of the land of Egypt, out of the house of bondage. Thou shalt have no other gods before me.	
II Thou shalt not make unto thee any graven image. . . . Thou shalt not bow down thyself to them, nor serve them: for I the Lord thy God am a jealous God. . . .	
III Thou shalt not take the name of the Lord thy God in vain.	
IV Remember the sabbath day, to keep it holy. Six days shalt thou labour and do all thy work.	
V Honour thy father and thy mother: that thy days may be long upon the land which the Lord thy God giveth thee.	
VI Thou shalt not kill.	
VII Thou shalt not commit adultery.	
VIII Thou shalt not steal.	
IX Thou shalt not bear false witness against thy neighbour.	
X Thou shalt not covet thy neighbour's house, thou shalt not covet thy neighbour's wife, nor his manservant, nor his maidservant, nor his ox, nor his ass, nor any thing that is thy neighbor's.	

I. HOLY PEOPLE (18:1–20:27)

A. Analysis

First read the three chapters in one sitting; then study each chapter separately. Here are some suggestions:
1. *Chapter 18*: Study the chapter in three parts: introduction (vv. 1-5); laws of moral defilement (vv. 6-23); summary (vv. 24-30). According to the introduction, what is the basic motivation for a believer's walk?

_____

_____

What other things do you learn from this paragraph?

_____

What other motivation is taught in the summary?

_____

2. *Chapter 19*: Here one of Leviticus's key verses appears (v. 2). (Read 1 Pet. 1:13-25 and observe how Peter applies this key verse of Leviticus.) Now study this verse in the light of the context of the entire chapter, observing especially two things: (1) repetition of the phrase "I am the Lord [your God]" (count the occurrences); (2) similarity of this chapter to the content of the Ten Commandments (Ex. 20). To complete this latter exercise, record on the following lines the similarities you observe:

_____

_____

_____

3. *Chapter 20*: Spend much time in the summary paragraph of verses 22-26. Make a list of the many universal spiritual truths taught here.

_____

_____

_____

_____

B. Comments

These chapters on personal habits show the dreadful depths to which fallen human nature is capable of sinking, including incest (chap. 18) and the horrible practice of offering children as human sacrifices to Molech, god of the Ammonites (18:21; 20:1-5; cf. 1 Kings 11:7). Human nature is the same throughout all ages. Read what Paul, inspired of the Holy Spirit, wrote about it in Romans 1:21-32. The depravity of man is boldly declared in God's Word.

A good practical lesson for Christians today is embodied in 18:1-5. There is a widespread notion that we should *conform* in some measure to the ways of those around us and not offend them even though we must thereby offend God. Read what Romans 12:2 says about this type of conforming. The Lord is our God, and we must obey *Him* regardless of what other people around us do.

II. HOLY PRIESTS (21:1–22:33)

The key phrase of these chapters is "I the Lord do sanctify them." Notice the various places where the phrase occurs. Observe that the regulations imposed on the priests were stricter than those on the people (shown in earlier chapters). This confirms the principle that responsibility is proportional to light and privilege. Read Luke 12:48. Compare the spiritual requirements of holy living of these groups today:

parent	———	child
teacher	———	pupil
minister	———	flock
leader	———	follower

Applications

To live a life pleasing to God a Christian must walk daily with God. This demands that his actions glorify God and that his motives behind the actions likewise glorify God.

List some of the prominent *deeds* and *motives* required of Christian laity and leaders alike that are taught by these chapters.

Lesson 7

Leviticus 23:1–25:55

Holy Times

An atmosphere of joy, rest, and celebration pervades these chapters, affording a thrilling climax to a book that is filled with rules and regulations. Tarry long over the chapters and let them teach you many precious things.

As we have already seen, Leviticus emphasizes the holiness of heart without which there can be no approach to, or walk with, God. God instituted these holy times in the calendar of the Israelites so that His people would set aside many days of each year especially to meditate over who He was and what He had done for them. The convocations had a wholesome positive purpose—to emphasize that believers were to be separated unto the Lord as well as separated from evil. And what the Israelites learned and experienced at these holy seasons they were to practice *daily*, step by step, throughout their lives.

A. Analysis

Read through the chapters at least twice before bringing together your observations. As you read, underline phrases in the text that stand out to you. Look especially for clues as to why God commanded the Israelites to observe these holy times.

Now record on the following chart your conclusions as to the major purpose of each celebration and the prominent truth revealed about God by each. The first item, Sabbath, is completed as an example. Use all the verses cited to help you in your conclusions.

HOLY TIMES   LEVITICUS 23-25

PASSAGES	HOLY TIME	DATE	MAIN PURPOSE OF THE OBSERVANCE	GOD SEEN AS:
Lev. 23:3 Ex. 20:8-11 Deut. 5:12-15	SABBATH	7th day (weekly)	Rest from labor; worship of God	Creator; Lord
Lev. 23:5 Num. 28:16 Deut. 16:1-2	PASSOVER	1/14		
Lev. 23:6-8 Num. 28:17-25 Deut. 16:3-8	UNLEAVENED BREAD*	1/15-21		
Lev. 23:9-14 Ex. 23:16 Num. 28:26-31	FIRSTFRUITS	1/16		
Lev. 23:15-22 Ex. 34:22 Deut. 16:9-12	PENTECOST* (Harvest; Weeks)	3/6		
Lev. 23:23-25 Num. 29:1-6	TRUMPETS	7/1		
Lev. 23:26-32 Lev. 16 Num. 29:7-11	DAY of ATONEMENT	7/10		
Lev. 23:33-44 Num. 29:12-40 Deut. 16:13-15	TABERNACLES*	7/15-21		
Lev. 25:1-7 Ex. 23:10-11	SABBATICAL YEAR	every 7th year		
Lev. 25:8-55	JUBILEE	every 50th year		

*Observe from Exodus 23:14-17 and Deuteronomy 16:16-17 that three times yearly all the men of Israel were to make pilgrimages to the place of worship and to observe these feasts.

1. *Sabbath.* The Old Testament Sabbath has been succeeded by the New Testament Lord's Day as the special day of worship for God's people. Compare the two days as to (1) the basic principles underlying them and (2) the event in history each commemorates.

_____

_____

_____

_____

2. *Passover.* What is the origin of the word "Passover"? (Read Ex. 12.)

_____

What was the key to Israel's deliverance?

_____

3. *Unleavened Bread.* This seven-day feast immediately followed the Passover celebration. What is the spiritual significance of this?

_____

4. *Firstfruits.* Read Romans 8:29; 1 Corinthians 15:20, 23; 16:15; James 1:18; and Revelation 14:4 to see the typical teaching of this feast.
5. *Pentecost.* The Holy Spirit was given to the church for a new ministry on the day the Jews were observing this holy day (Acts 2:1). Is any typical truth taught by this feast?

_____

6. *Trumpets.* The trumpets were for announcement. Observe that this was the beginning of the seventh month. What did the number *seven* usually symbolize in Old Testament days?

_____

Considering the holy times observed in this month, how did the month take on special significance?

_____

_____

7. *Day of Atonement.* Recall from your previous study the significance of this important day. Was it a day of mere commemoration or a day when God actually worked salvation?

---

8. Tabernacles. Observe that this was a feast of rejoicing (23:40). Contrast this with the Day of Atonement. Over what were the Israelites to rejoice? (23:43).

(Note: The booths of this feast symbolized the temporary dwellings of tents of the wilderness journey. The word "Tabernacles" of v. 34 refers to these booths.)
9. *Sabbatical Year.* The Sabbath day was a day of rest for the Israelites. The sabbatical year intended rest for what?

---

10. *Jubilee.* What was God teaching the Israelites through this observance? Note a key phrase in 25:23.

Before reading the comments of the next section, write out a list of the spiritual lessons you have learned from these chapters. Are you persuaded that it is possible for you to live the life God wants you to live?

B. Comments

It is interesting to observe the similarities of these holy days and seasons to key events in the calendar of the present New Testament age. Before reading any further, study the chart of the Hebrew calendar on pages 62-63.

1. *Feast of the Passover.* Each year the Israelites celebrated their redemption from death and bondage in Egypt by this Passover feast. Then came Christ, the spotless Lamb of God, and on the anniversary of the Passover (cf. John 12:1) He died on the cross, thereby redeeming us from spiritual death and bondage and becoming our great Passover (1 Cor. 5:7).

2. *Feast of the Unleavened Bread.* This feast, closely connected with the Passover, was often counted as a part of it. The purpose of the first Passover in Egypt was to bring the Israelites into a

new spiritual relationship with their Lord, a relationship they acknowledged by partaking of this feast. The purpose of Christ's death was to bring people into fellowship with God, and if His death could not have accomplished this, it would have been a failure.

3. *Feast of the Firstfruits.* This feast marked the beginning of the grain harvest, the fruit of the land. Note that it occurred "on the morrow after the sabbath" (Lev. 23:10-11). Christ, the Firstfruits of "them that slept [died]" (1 Cor. 15:20-23), was raised from the dead on the morrow after the Sabbath (Matt. 28:1).

4. *Feast of Pentecost.* Note carefully that this feast occurred fifty days (the word "Pentecost" comes from the Greek *pentēkostē*, meaning "fiftieth") after the Feast of the Firstfruits. After Christ's resurrection The disciples waited in the "upper room" until the day of Pentecost was fully come—ten days—and then on the anniversary of this feast the Holy Spirit descended upon them and the church was born. (Read Acts 2:1, 1 Cor. 10:16-17; 12:13, 20.)

The above four feasts occurred in the first part of the Jewish year, even as the events they typify occurred in the first part of this present age. The holy times that appeared later in the year are seen by some Bible scholars to typify events of the last days, thus:

5. *Feast of Trumpets.* This may be prophetic of the future regathering of Israel. Read Isaiah 18:3, 7; 27:12-13; 48:1-14; Joel 2:15-32.

6. *Day of Atonement.* In Romans 11 Paul clearly teaches that Israel has a place in the future. When he writes, "And so all Israel shall be saved," he dates this salvation as the time when God "shall take away their sins" (Rom. 11:26-27). The Day of Atonement in Israel's religious calendar appropriately pointed to Israel's final day of salvation, when the nation would accept Jesus as their Messiah. (Read Deut. 30:1-10; Rom. 11:1-36.)

7. *Feast of* Tabernacles. Here is Israel at rest in the Kingdom after the nation's regathering and restoration. (Read Ezra 3:4; Zech. 14:16-19; Rev. 21:3.)

8. *Year of Jubilee.* Every seventh day was a sabbatic day, every seventh year was a sabbatic year, and every forty-nine (seven-times-seven) years there was a jubilee. This jubilee well typifies the millennial glory. It must have been a glorious time in Israel when, in the fiftieth year, at the sounding of the trumpet on the Day of Atonement, slaves were loosed from bondage, captives were set free, debtors liberated, exiles returned home, and the poor got back their possessions. From verses 14-16 of this chapter we see that all their business relations and dealing with others were regulated with reference to this year.

HEBREW CALENDAR

ORDER IN SACRED CALENDAR	ORDER IN CIVIL CALENDAR	PREEXILIC NAME	POSTEXILIC NAME	EQUIVALENT	SEASON	FARMING	FESTIVALS	BIBLICAL REFERENCES
1	(7)	Abib	NISAN	Mar.-Apr.	Spring Equinox Latter rains	Barley harvest begins Flax harvest	(1: RELIGIOUS NEW YEAR'S DAY, Num. 28:11) 14: Passover (Ex. 12:18) 15:21: Unleavened Bread (Lev. 23:6) 16: Firstfruits (Lev. 23:10 ff.)	Ex. 12:2 Neh. 2:1
2	(8)	Ziw	IYYAR	Apr.-May	Summer Dry season begins	Barley harvest	14: Later Passover (Num. 9:10-11)	1 Kings 6:1, 37
3	(9)		SIVAN	May-June		Wheat harvest begins Early figs ripen	6: Pentecost (Lev. 23:15-21)	Esther 8:9
4	(10)		TAMMUZ	June-July		Wheat harvest Grape harvest		Ezek. 8:14
5	(11)		AB	July-Aug.		Principal fruit month: grape, fig, olive		
6	(12)		ELUL	Aug.-Sept.		Dates and summer figs		Neh. 6:15

#	()	Name	Name	Months	Season	Agriculture	Feasts / Notes	Reference
7	(1)	Etanim	TISHRI	Sept.-Oct.	Early Rains Seedtime	(Plowing and sowing)	(1: CIVIL NEW YEAR'S DAY) 1: Trumpets (Lev. 23:24; Num. 29:1) 10: Day of Atonement (Lev. 16:29ff.) 15-21: Feast of Tabernacles (Lev. 23:34ff.)	1 Kings 8:2
8	(2)	Bul	HESHVAN	Oct.-Nov.		Wheat and barley sowing	22: Solemn Assembly (Lev. 23:36)	1 Kings 6:38
9	(3)		KISLEV	Nov.-Dec.	Winter begins (John 10:22)		25: Feast of Dedication (Lights) (John 10:22)	Neh. 1:1
10	(4)		TEBETH	Dec.-Jan.	Rainy winter months	Cultivation of Jordan Valley begins		Esther 2:16
11	(5)		SHEBAT	Jan.-Feb.		Almond blossoms Oranges ripen		Zech. 1:7
12	(6)		ADAR	Feb.-Mar.		Barley ripens Citrus fruit harvest		Ezra 6:15
13			ADAR SHENI	Intercalary month:		Added each year that the barley was not ripe on the 16th of Nisan. Two such years were not allowed in succession.		

This joyous year of jubilee reminds us of a great day coming when at the sounding of the trumpet great things shall take place: the dead in Christ shall rise first; then we which are alive and remain shall be caught up to meet the Lord in the air. Slaves shall be loosed from bondage, captives set free, debtors liberated, and we shall enter into the joy of our inheritance. If we are looking for this great day, can we be much engrossed with the things of this world? Will not this anticipation regulate our conduct in regard to this life and our dealings with others?

C. A Concluding Study

Earlier in this lesson it was observed that there was a wholesome, positive purpose for the convocations, emphasizing that believers were to be separated unto the Lord, as well as separated from evil. As a concluding project for this lesson, record on the accompanying chart what each feast taught about the two facets of separation.

THE HOLY TIMES	SEPARATION	
	UNTO THE LORD	FROM EVIL
SABBATH		
PASSOVER		
UNLEAVENED BREAD		
FIRSTFRUITS		
PENTECOST		
TRUMPETS		
DAY OF ATONEMENT		
TABERNACLE		
SABBATICAL YEAR		
JUBILEE		

Lesson 8 *Leviticus 26:1–27:34*

Just Recompense and Holy Vows

Whereas chapters 23 to 25 serve as a climactic section in the structure of the book of Leviticus, chapters 26 and 27 bring the book to a conclusion with appropriate themes, as the present study will reveal. The accompanying outline shows how the preceding chapters are related to the chapters of this lesson.

18	21	23	26	27
HOLY PEOPLE	HOLY PRIESTS	HOLY TIMES	JUST RECOMPENSE	HOLY VOWS
THE WALK WITH GOD				

I. JUST RECOMPENSE (26:1-46)

A. Survey

This chapter reminds the reader that there is such a sobering fact as the inevitable *consequences* of life's decisions and actions. No one can escape the divine law of returns. Paul stated this succinctly when he wrote, "Whatsoever a man soweth, that shall he also reap" (Gal. 6:7).

The entire book of Leviticus has set forth God's many statutes, judgments, and laws that the opening paragraph of chapter 26 (vv. 1-2) now summarizes by way of citing only a few of the major ones. (This is a literary device known as synecdoche, where a part is made to represent the whole—a common device in the Old Testament.) In the verses that follow the opening paragraph (vv. 3-45) God tells His people the consequences of observing His laws and the consequences of refusing to obey. The last verse of the chapter is taken by some to serve as the natural conclusion of Leviticus, with chapter 27 as an appendix.

B. Analysis

Keeping the above survey in mind, pursue your own independent study of this chapter. First read the chapter through twice, underlining key words and phrases in your Bible as you read.

Notice how this chapter is organized, as shown by the accompanying analytical chart (p. 66). Mark the paragraph divisions in your Bible, if necessary.

1. Record on the chart some of the key words and phrases you have noted.

2. Observe the progression in intensity of judgments of the section 26:14-39.

3. From what you may already know of the Babylonian captivity (586 B.C.), how were verses 27-39 fulfilled at that time?

_____

_____

_____

4. What do you learn about confession and covenant from verses 40-45?

_____

_____

_____

C. Applications

Make a list of sobering practical lessons that Christians can learn from this chapter.

_____

_____

_____

_____

JUST RECOMPENSE
LEVITICUS 26

(Introductory paragraph)	1	
	3 If . . . Then . . .	BLESSINGS for OBEDIENCE

	14 But if . . .
	     (Then) . . .
	
	18 If
	    Then
	
	21 If
	    Then
	
	23 If
	    Then
	
	27 If
	    Then
		JUDGMENTS
		for DISOBEDIENCE

	40 If they shall confess . . . Then will I remember	RESTORATION for CONFESSION
(Concluding verse)	46	

II. HOLY VOWS (27:1-34)

The special vows about which the Lord spoke in this chapter were over and above the requirements He laid down in all the previous chapters. For this reason the chapter is appropriately located at the end of the book, as if to remind believers that if they ever consider themselves to have arrived in this life at a mountain peak of maturity, there are still higher mountains to conquer. (Read Phil. 3:12.)

A. Background

Before you study this chapter, acquaint yourself with the following background and definitions as orientation to your study:

1. These vows were special ("singular," 27:2) vows, not the usual acts of worship. No one was compelled to make a vow, but once the vow was made, its regulations had to be followed. (Read Deut. 23:22-23; Prov. 20:25; Eccles. 5:3-5.)

2. The vows were acts of devotion by which gifts were assigned to God. The person making the vow usually did so to seek the Lord's blessing on himself or his possessions, through protection in danger or distress or through success and well-being. Whatever was given to the Lord in this moment of devotion continued to be His, in a legal sense, until the period of the vow terminated. At such a time the original owner could usually recover ("redeem") his title to the gift by making a prescribed payment to the sanctuary. The amount of payment was usually 20 percent over and above the priest's estimation on the value of the item (beast, field, house, etc.).

3. An actual tangible transaction apparently did not take place in the case of vowing a person. That is, the person who was vowed did not, for example, enter into the employment of the sanctuary as a servant. A man so vowing himself or a member of his household was giving such a gift to the Lord only in a legal sense, not in a real sense. Then at the end of the period of the vow (there apparently was a temporal terminus to such a vow) the person was redeemed from that legal transfer by the payment of a price to the priest.

4. Two major benefits of these special vows were: (1) the person making the vow was reminded of the ever present privilege of voluntarily dedicating himself and his possessions to God; and (2) the material needs of the ministry of the sanctuary were helped by the donations of redemption money.

5. How this opportunity for deep devotion to God was usurped in later centuries by those legalists who violated its intent

is illustrated by Mark 7:9-13. Read these verses before reading the following commentary: "The law concerning duty to parents was plain, but the Jews, with characteristic sophistry, had devised a means of evading it, even under the cloak of piety. A son could pledge his money to be paid into the temple treasury. This could be done in an ideal sense without any actual payment being made, or the payment could be deferred until after his death. He could even do it in a fit of anger, and could then tell his old parents in their time of need that he could offer them no help, since his money was *Corban*, i.e., dedicated under oath. *Corban* is a transliteration of a Hebrew word meaning an offering or gift devoted to God."[1]

B. Analysis

First read through the chapter twice, observing such things as key words, key phrases, and groupings of content. The following questions and comments will help you:
1. *Persons* (vv. 1-8). Why the different redemption prices according to age and sex?

_____

_____

_____

What do you see of *grace* in the provision of verse 8?

_____

_____

2. *Beasts* (vv. 9-13). Observe from verses 9 and 10 that a beast that qualified for the altar sacrifice was an outright gift to the sanctuary, not redeemable. What provision was made for other kinds of beasts? (vv. 11-13).

_____

_____

3. *Houses* (vv. 14-15). Notice that the rules of redemption for houses were the same as those for unclean beasts (vv. 11-13).
4. *Fields* (vv. 16-25). The rules concerning sanctifying fields were rather complicated. (Refer to a commentary, if necessary, for

---

1. F. Davidson et al., eds., *The New Bible Commentary* (Grand Rapids: Eerdmans, 1953), p. 820.

further help on this paragraph.) The estimation of redemption price was basically according to what? (v. 16).

In light of this, why would a landowner be anxious to dedicate his land to God, in terms of receiving God's blessing?

Observe that the year of jubilee came into the rules of this vow. What happened to land in the year of jubilee?

Who really owned the land?

5. *Firstlings and devoted things* (vv. 26-29). This paragraph is devoted to things unredeemable. Why were the firstlings (firstborn) of clean cattle exempt from this dedication? (cf. Ex. 13:1-2).

The "devoted" (means here "banned") things of verses 28-29 were things that, because of some related transgression, had actually already been put under a ban as far as man's use was concerned. In that sense they were surrendered or handed over to God, who after all is owner of all things. Of this C. F. Keil says, "The owner of cattle and fields was only allowed to put them under the ban when they had been either desecrated by idolatry or abused by unholy purposes. For there can be no doubt that the idea which lay at the foundation of the ban was that of a compulsory dedication of something which resisted or impeded sanctification."[2] (Note: "banned" and "devoted" are translated from the same Hebrew word, *herem*.)

6. *Tithes* (vv. 30-33; 34 is a concluding verse). Why were vows not made over tithes? (v. 30).

2. C. F. Keil and F. Delitzsch, *Commentaries on the Old Testament* (Grand Rapids: Eerdmans, 1949) 2:485.

Compare this with the case of firstlings (v. 26).

Observe that a man could buy back some of that which he had given as tithes (beasts, etc.) by paying the valued price plus 20 percent. This provision was made in view of the procedure described in verses 32-33. It was customary to designate which cattle would be given as tithe in this manner: the animals were led in single file out of an enclosure, as they were counted by the shepherd holding a rod; and each tenth animal was marked by the rod, which had been dipped in some coloring substance. This tenth animal had to be given to the Lord—whether it was good or bad. But the owner had the option of recovering any choice cattle so designated, availing himself of the privilege cited in verse 31.

Read Genesis 14:20; 28:22, and Hebrews 7:5-9, for the only other references to tithes of an earlier date than this law of Leviticus 27. Despite the fact that tithes were not frequently mentioned (nor recorded as part of the legislation) before this time, the wording of Leviticus 27:30 is such that it may be correctly assumed that the tithes were well known by this time.

Why would a paragraph about tithes be a wholesome last thought in the book of Leviticus?

C. Applications

Why did God make provision for such acts of devotion in the life of the Israelites?

What Christian truths can you learn from this concluding chapter of Leviticus?

D. Summary

Leviticus was Israel's handbook of worship and daily living. In this book the people were taught the stark truth that only holy people can have intimate communion with a holy God. They learned how such communion was possible through:

1. Acceptable offerings	(heart of the believer)	(1–7)
2. Priestly services	(help to the believer)	(8–10)
3. Purity and separation	(habitat of the believer)	(11–15)
4. Atoning blood	(hope of the believer)	(16–17)
5. Righteous walk	(habits of the believer)	(18–22)
6. Holy convocations	(holidays of the believer)	(23–25).

The richest and deepest truths of Leviticus are those of its prophetic types which point to the glorious Person and word of Jesus Christ. In Leviticus Christ is seen as the offering, the offerer, and the priest—all three—and in so being and doing He can rightly claim to be "the way, the truth, and the life" (John 14:6).

Lesson 9
New Testament
Use of Leviticus

In some of the earlier lessons you have been directed to the epistle to the Hebrews to see how Christ fulfilled many of the types of Leviticus. The study of this lesson is intended to introduce you to all the verses of the New Testament that are actual verbal allusions to either the Hebrew or the Greek Septuagint texts of Leviticus.

Inasmuch as it is vital for a comparative study like this to have all the text before you at one time, it is suggested that you record for each reference at least the key phrase and sufficient context to show the connection between the New Testament and Leviticus verses.

NEW TESTAMENT ALLUSIONS TO LEVITICUS

LEVITICUS	NEW TESTAMENT
5:11	Luke 2:24
7:12	Hebrews 13:15
11:44	1 Peter 1:16
12:1-8	Luke 2:22
12:8	Luke 2:24
13:49	Matthew 8:4
	Mark 1:44
	Luke 17:14

LEVITICUS	NEW TESTAMENT
14:2-3	Luke 17:14
16:2, 12	Hebrews 6:19
	Revelation 8:5
16:27	Hebrews 13:11,13
17:7	1 Corinthians 10:20
18:5	Luke 10:28
	Romans 10:5
	Galatians 3:12
19:2	Matthew 5:48
	1 Peter 1:16
19:12	Matthew 5:33
19:13	James 5:4
19:18	Matthew 5:43
	Matthew 19:19
	Matthew 22:39
	Mark 12:31
	Luke 10:27
	Romans 12:19
	Romans 13:9
	Galatians 5:14
	James 2:8

LEVITICUS	NEW TESTAMENT
20:7	1 Peter 1:16
23:29	Acts 3:23
24:9	Matthew 12:4 Mark 2:26 Luke 6:4
24:19-20	Matthew 5:38
25:10	Luke 4:19
26:12	2 Corinthians 6:16
26:21	Revelation 15:1 Revelation 15:6 Revelation 15:8 Revelation 21:9

Some observations that you will want to make in this comparative verse study center on these things:

1. "Prophecies" of Leviticus fulfilled in the New Testament
2. Timeless universal principles reiterated and applied in the New Testament
3. Truths of Leviticus advanced and expanded in the New Testament
4. Laws and commandments obeyed in the New Testament

Write out your observations and the conclusions you have arrived at from this study.

Lesson 10
Review Questions

Now that you have come to the close of your study of Leviticus, it will be very helpful to you to go back over the entire book and review its highlights and prominent teachings.

Before answering the questions below you may want to quickly thumb through the pages of this manual to refresh your memory on the paths of study you have taken.

Spend sufficient time on each question. Give concise but adequate answers. If you need help on any question, refer back to the Bible and to the appropriate lesson of the manual.

1. In your own words, what does Leviticus contribute to the volume of the Bible? Your answer should reveal the main theme and purposes of the book.

_____

_____

_____

_____

2. See how much of the survey chart of Leviticus you can reproduce. Show the various outlines and the chapter locations of the major divisions.

3. Name what you consider to be ten of the key words of Leviticus.

_____

_____

_____

_____

_____

4. Name the five principal offerings.

_____

_____

_____

_____

_____

5. What was the dominant characteristic of each offering?

_____

_____

_____

_____

_____

6. How was each of the five offerings fulfilled in Christ?

_____

_____

_____

_____

7. What principles for Christians today are taught by the consecration ceremonies of Aaron and his sons?

_____

_____

_____

8. What main truth is taught by the story of the sin of Nadab and Abihu?

_____

_____

9. Recall as much as you can of the procedures of ceremony on the Day of Atonement.

_____

_____

_____

_____

10. How does Christ fulfill the types of the ceremonies of the Day of Atonement?

_____

_____

_____

_____

11. What are some of the major lessons taught by the laws of the clean and unclean?

_____

_____

_____

12. What does Leviticus teach about separation? holiness? dedication?

_____

_____

_____

_____

_____

13. What may be learned about Christian leadership from Leviticus?

_____

_____

_____

14. Name the holy times of chapters 23–25.

_____

_____

_____

_____

_____

_____

_____

_____

_____

15. What was the main characteristic of each convocation, and what are the practical truths taught here?

_____

_____

_____

_____

_____

_____

_____

_____

16. What does Leviticus teach about just recompense?

_____

17. What may be learned about God and about man from this book?

_____

_____

_____

_____

_____

18. Write out a list of some of the blessings you have received from your study of this portion of God's Word.

_____

_____

_____

_____

Bibliography

RESOURCES FOR FURTHER STUDY

Douglas, James D., ed. *The New Bible Dictionary*. Grand Rapids: Eerdmans, 1962.

Fairbairn, P. *The Typology of Scripture*. Grand Rapids: Zondervan, n.d.

Jensen, Irving L. *Jensen's Survey of the Old Testament*. Chicago: Moody, 1978.

The New International Version Study Edition. Grand Rapids: Zondervan, 1985.

The Ryrie Study Bible. Chicago: Moody, 1978.

Sprink, James F. *Types and Shadows of Christ in the Tabernacle*. New York: Loizeaux, 1946.

Strong, James. *The Exhaustive Concordance of the Bible*. New York: Abingdon, 1890.

Tenney, Merrill C., ed. *The Zondervan Pictorial Bible Dictionary*. Grand Rapids: Zondervan, n.d.

Unger, Merrill F. *The New Unger's Bible Dictionary*. Chicago: Moody, 1988.

―――――. *The New Unger's Bible Handbook*. Chicago: Moody, 1984.

COMMENTARIES AND TOPICAL STUDIES

Allis, Oswald T. *God Spake by Moses*. Philadelphia: Presby. and Ref., 1951.

―――――. "Leviticus." In *The New Bible Commentary*, ed. F. Davidson, A. M. Stibbs, and E. F. Kevan. Grand Rapids: Eerdmans, 1953.

Bonar, Andrew A. *A Commentary on the Book of Leviticus*. Grand Rapids: Zondervan, 1959.

Erdman, Charles R. *The Book of Leviticus.* New York: Revell, 1951.

Gardiner, Frederic. "Leviticus." In *Lange's Commentary on the Holy Scriptures,* by J. P. Lange. Grand Rapids: Zondervan, n.d.

Harrison, Roland. *Leviticus, an Introduction and Commentary.* Downers Grove: InterVarsity, 1980.

Heslop, W. G. *Lessons from Leviticus.* Grand Rapids: Baker, 1945.

Ironside, H. A. *Lectures on the Levitical Offerings.* New York: Loizeaux, 1929.

Kellogg, Samuel H. *The Book of Leviticus.* New York: George H. Doran, n.d.

Mackintosh, C. F. *Notes on the Book of Leviticus.* New York: Loizeaux, n.d.

Coleman, Robert, "Leviticus." In *The Wycliffe Bible Commentary.* Edited by Charles F. Pfeiffer and Everett F. Harrison. Chicago: Moody, 1962.